Ready or Not

Ready or Not
Tips for the New Grad

A Gift for Graduates

Lisa J. Shultz

*"It is time to start living
the life you've imagined."*
~ Henry James

*Dedicated to
Summer and Liberty
And all graduates
as they spread their wings and fly!*

To:_____

From:_____

Message:

_____
_____
_____
_____
_____
_____
_____
_____
_____
_____
_____

CONTENTS

Introduction. 15

Health. 17
Finances and Work. 25
Play and Leisure. 39
Mind. 47
Relationships and Love. 63
Spirit. 77
Community and Service. 97
And a Few More. 103

Notes. 145
101 Things I Want to Do 149
Recommended Reading. 159

Acknowledgments 164
About Lisa. 165

INTRODUCTION

*"Believe nothing. No matter where you read it,
or who said it, even if I have said it,
unless it agrees with your own reason
and your own common sense."*
~Buddha

As my two daughters approached graduation, I began to wonder if I had instilled in them the virtues and principles that I felt were important to their lives, especially in moving from the security of our home to the big world of employment, relationships, and life overall.

I felt a need to review and remind them of what really mattered. I reflected upon my own experiences—the good parts as well as the not-so-good. I thought about what I wished I had known as a young person, what I had learned the hard way, and what had worked well for me.

I also reviewed some classic books that had positively influenced me along the way. I integrated my own experience and opinions with suggestions from friends and family and combined that with the teachings of many authors and leaders, both past and present. In several cases, I took complex topics and extracted a few key sentences that summarized their view. If a point is not immediately understandable, the recommended reading list will expand upon those subjects.

It is my hope that my daughters and you, the reader of this book, will refer to this book throughout your life. My hope, in adding the section for your 101 Dream List entries at the end of the book, is that you will continue to use your list by adding to it as you connect with more of your dreams. Occasionally review what you've recorded and take time to reflect on your progress.

I suggest that you review these tips at least yearly, perhaps around the time of your birthday. This is often a good time to contemplate what has transpired over the prior year and set intentions for the upcoming one.

My intention is that this book will have a positive ripple effect for all who read and apply its wisdom. I have put my heart and soul into its creation, and I hope it will act as a guide toward an abundant and happy life for you.

Cheers to your success,

Lisa J. Shultz

HEALTH

*"To insure good health:
eat lightly, breathe deeply,
live moderately, cultivate cheerfulness,
and maintain an interest in life."
~ William Londen*

Practice Prevention

You will save a great deal of money
and experience a higher
quality of life as you grow older,
if you practice prevention.
Eat healthy food, exercise,
use sunscreen, and practice moderation
to prevent problems from
occurring down the road.
Study the lives of people who
have achieved 100+ years of age.
Learn how they have lived
and what they have done
to take care of themselves.

Stretch and Exercise Your Body

Keep your body flexible,
strong, and looking good.
Engage in a sport
or activity that keeps
you in shape.
Take lots of walks.

Drink Water

Make water
your primary beverage.
Drink a glass of water
first thing in the morning.
Drink water consistently
all day long.
Cultivate a love of water.

Eat Natural
and Nutrient Rich Food

Eat lots of fruit
and vegetables every day.
Whenever possible,
eat food that is closest to nature.
Avoid processed and fast foods,
additives and dyes.
Buy and eat organic
whenever possible.
Support farmers and ranchers
who practice healthy
and humane treatment
of the animals you consume.

Brush Your Teeth

Keep your teeth clean
and gums healthy by brushing
your teeth several times a day
and flossing your teeth once a day.
See a dental professional
twice a year for a check-up and cleaning,
and take good care of your smile.

Get Plenty of Sleep

Allow your body to get
a good night's sleep.
Go to bed early sometimes.
Take a nap sometimes.
Make getting enough sleep
a priority for good health.

Say No to Drugs and Smoking

Smoking and drugs harm
your health and are addictive.
Even caffeine, whether in coffee,
soda, or energy drinks, is addictive
and is sometimes found
to be lethal in high doses.
Drugs diminish vitality and awareness.
Drugs lead to heartache
and sometimes death.

FINANCES AND WORK

*"The philosophy of the rich
versus the poor is this:
The rich invest their money
and spend what is left;
the poor spend their money
and invest what is left."
~Jim Rohn*

Develop the Habit of Saving Money

Have a plan to save a
percentage of all money you earn,
inherit, win, or receive as a gift.
Lay this amount aside
to grow for your future
financial independence.
Create a mechanism to set
aside savings each month.
Have your money growing
and working for you.

Hire a Financial Planner

Even if you are not earning
much money and have debt,
hire a financial planner to guide
you out of debt, grow your savings,
and discuss investment options.
Consult frequently with this advisor,
as your life changes with new jobs,
marriage, kids, and the changing
financial environments.
Visit with your advisor
once a year, and study
your investments once a quarter.
Don't make major financial decisions
without first meeting with your advisor.

Use a Credit Card with Caution

It is best to use cash or debit card,
unless you can pay off your
credit card in full each month.
If you are a spender,
avoid using a credit card
until you become a saver.
Then use your credit card
only when absolutely necessary.

Avoid Debt and Pay It Off

It is difficult to ever get ahead
and feel free when chained to debt.
If you have been fortunate to graduate
without debt, keep your new life
as debt-free as possible.
If you do have debt upon
graduation, have a plan
to pay it off as soon as possible.
Meet with a financial
planner to create your plan.
Save up for special purchases.
Live a frugal life until your
income allows larger purchases.

Create a Budget

A budget will help you realize
how much money you spend on
clothing, technology, recreation,
entertainment, and dining out
compared to necessities of rent
and housing, utilities, food,
promotion of health, and medical.
A budget will show you what you
can afford and what will have to wait.
Understanding the difference between
what you really need and what you want
can assist you to shop wisely.
Postpone purchases when possible,
to assure your savings plan
is always the priority.

Live Below Your Means

Don't try to keep up with
your neighbors next door.
Just because you get a raise, promotion,
or a new job, avoid going out to
buy a bigger house, fancier car,
or the latest TV.
With a bigger house,
you will have more expenses,
more furniture to buy, and
more space to clean, heat, or cool.
Consider whether you really need
more space and whether your budget
and savings plan can support
the upgrade.
Upsize with caution.
Downsizing brings freedom,
and upsizing requires
more responsibility.

Delay Buying Luxury Items

If you have saved each month
for your future in a special
investment account and you
have paid all your bills in full,
and then you have some money still
left over, place that money into
an account for a future luxury item.
When you have saved enough
to pay for that luxury item in full,
then buy it.
Immediate gratification
is not your friend.
Delayed gratification
can be your best friend.

Avoid Lending Money to Friends

If you lend money to friends,
it will forever change your friendship.
And there is a good chance
you will never be repaid.
The weight of the loan creates
tension in the relationship
psychologically, and saying no
may save the friendship ultimately.
On the flip side, avoid asking
friends to loan you money.

Buy Used Cars

Buying used cars
is a great way to save money.
New cars drop
in value almost immediately
after you buy them.
Buying a used car
that is a couple of years old is often
the best use of your car money.
Buying the car in full and
avoiding car payments is a
worthy goal.
Drive the car
for as long as possible
by maintaining it well.

Develop the Habit of Doing More Than You Are Paid For

If you love your work,
you can sustain countless
hours without fatigue.
Find work you love and then
give to it more than is expected.
In time, your effort will be
rewarded in more money
and satisfaction as well as an
excellent reputation, which will
bring you more opportunities.

Keep Gift Giving to a Minimum

Commercialism around the holidays has gotten ridiculous.
Do you really need to buy someone a present for every little holiday?
Could you instead spend quality time, create a gift by hand, or give food, flowers, or a plant?
Celebrating time with family and friends over a meal or an activity rather than gift giving can ease your financial outlay and keep clutter from accumulating as well.

Tithe

In addition to saving a percentage
of what you earn, tithing (giving money)
to a person, organization, church,
or cause that has meaning to you
keeps money flowing.
Money that comes in and is saved,
spent wisely, and also given to
a worthy person or entity, keeps energy
flowing instead of stagnant.
Money given out with love
and gratitude often comes back to you
in larger quantities down the road.

PLAY AND LEISURE

"Just play. Have fun.
Enjoy the game."
~Michael Jordan

Play

Play a game,
play an instrument,
play a sport.
Play with a child
or a pet.
Play with an elderly person.
Be playful with a partner.
Take breaks from work to play.

Smile

Smile as much as possible
all day long.
Smile at strangers you pass.
Smile at those you love
while looking at them
directly in their eyes.
Smile in photographs.
Enjoy smiling.

Laugh

Laugh at yourself.
Laugh in groups.
Find the humor
and the funny side of things.
Watch movies that
make you laugh.
See if you can
make someone else laugh.

Sing

Sing your favorite songs.
Sing in the shower.
Sing while driving.
Sing with other people.

Dance

Dance to your favorite song.
Slow dance with someone you love.
Dance with friends.
Take dancing lessons.
Dance for joy!

Plan Vacations and Take Them

Take trips to beautiful places,
natural parks, monuments,
historical places,
and places with a different
way of living or culture.
Expand your view of the world
through travel.

MIND

*"Whatever the mind can
conceive and believe,
it can achieve."
~Napoleon Hill*

Think Positive

Thoughts are real forces,
so choose your thoughts wisely.
Positive thoughts create a
positive vibration of energy
around you, which attracts
people and circumstances to you
that match those thoughts.

Recite Affirmations

Say positive affirmations daily.
Create a list of affirmations
that support your goals
and life directions.
Write your affirmations on paper,
a notecard, or journal.

Visualize

Visualize your dreams
and goals daily.
Create a vision board
or dream notebook.
See yourself in vivid detail
with the end result
you wish to have.
Imagine yourself as successful.
Dwell on every detail
of what the end result will look like.

Set Goals

Create specific goals for all
aspects of your life.
Goals that stretch your comfort zone
and get you excited are ideal.
Have at least one BIG goal
that would represent a quantum leap
or breakthrough in your life.
Write your goals down in a notebook
or notecards and review daily.

Create a Definiteness of Purpose

Discover and develop a passion,
and center all your activities
and decisions on it.
Cultivate a burning desire
to achieve your objective.
You then become a magnet
that attracts everything
that harmonizes with that purpose.

Make Plans

Create a plan to meet
your objectives.
What will you do today,
this week, this month,
this year to move closer to
your goals step-by-step?
Put your plans on paper.

Take Action

Act in spite of fear.
Be courageous.
Go for it.
Just do it.
Be proactive.

Be Enthusiastic

Find what you love to do
and do it enthusiastically.
Enthusiasm energizes your body.
It attracts people
and opportunities to you.
Enthusiasm is contagious.

Use Your Imagination

Rearrange ideas in different
ways to create new and improved
methods for doing things.
Weave new combinations of ideas
together to make something better.

Be More Concerned with Your Thoughts Than How Something Will Happen

Spend more time with focused,
positive thoughts than worry
or concern about how you will
achieve your goals.
With your mind clearly
focused in a positive way on your
ultimate, desired end result,
the right people, circumstances, and
events will present themselves
to you in alignment with your
most prevalent thoughts.

Read Books

Develop a love
of books and reading.
Read biographies
and teachings
of amazing people.
Read about history.
Read the works
of inspirational people.
Read a good story.

Always Find the Silver Lining or Lesson in Every Situation

Take responsibility for your
part in every situation.
Learn from it, let it go, and move on.
Defeat is temporary.
Opportunities are present
everywhere, even in what
appears to be a failure.
Ask yourself what you
need to do differently next time
to get a better result.
Look for the hidden treasure
of learning from the experience.
Things happen for a reason,
and that reason is there to serve you.

Rise Above Obstacles

Believe that you are
bigger than any obstacle.
Learn how to recover from setbacks.
Seek support to move past an obstacle.
Learn from the obstacle.
Correct yourself and continue.
Be unstoppable!

Don't Worry

Worry causes health problems
and takes away your
vital energy and creativity.
Most things that you are afraid
might happen never do.
Change your thoughts when
worry creeps in
to positive visualizations
or definitive action steps.

Take Complete Responsibility for Your Life

You are 100% responsible for
every aspect of your life.
Be willing to assume responsibility for
your mistakes and shortcomings.
Avoid blaming other people,
especially your parents, your childhood,
the government, the economy,
or any other outside circumstance
beyond yourself.
Your present experience of life
has been determined by the choices
you have already made.
Drop excuses and stories
and let go of being a victim.
You create everything
that happens in your life.
Own your own life.

RELATIONSHIPS AND LOVE

*"If civilization is to survive,
we must cultivate the science of
human relationships—the ability of
all peoples, of all kinds, to live together,
in the same world at peace."
~Franklin D. Roosevelt*

Hug

Hug your parents
and grandparents.
Hug your friends.
Hug your pets.
Make hugging a part
of your everyday life.

Choose Your Friends Wisely

Your income tends to
be the average of your five
closest friends.
Your friends can support you
or bring you down,
so hang out with positive people
who love life.
Sometimes you might need to find
new friends, unless the ones you have
are there for you in a positive way.

Don't Make Assumptions

Most assumptions
are completely inaccurate.
Whenever possible,
ask the person directly what they
meant when they said or did something.
Direct conversation is always better
than email or text,
which can be badly misinterpreted.
Incorrect assumptions
can cause unnecessary upset
and resentments.
Clear up confusion
promptly with direct questions.

Avoid Criticizing Others

Criticism stings and often
leads to lasting resentment.
Learn to appreciate the qualities
of others and give voice to what
is good and what is right and
leave criticism behind you.
Discover what you can
learn from others.

Be Honest and Open

Speak your truth
with compassion.
Be open to new ways
of looking at things and doing them.
Have honesty as a shared value
in your relationships.

Create Win-Win Deals

In all you do with business and life,
look for ways to have
each party or person win.
If there is no win-win,
do not continue.

Avoid Arguments

You can't win an argument,
even if you think you have won,
because you will lose the goodwill
of the other person.
When you are wrong,
admit it quickly.
Learn to apologize
and practice forgiveness.

Be a Good Listener

Talk less and listen more.
While listening to someone,
look them straight in the eyes
and give them your full attention.
Ask them questions
about what they are saying.
Encourage people
to talk about themselves.

Don't Worry About What Other People Think About You

What others think about you
is none of your business.
People tend to think about themselves
and not about you.
Follow your heart
and base your decisions
on your objectives and desires
and not the goals or
judgments of others.

Avoid Gossip and Judgment

Do not engage in idle gossip.
If you want to talk about people,
share their successes,
how they inspire you,
or what you have learned from them.
If you cannot say something
positive about a person,
refrain from saying anything at all.
Often your judgments of others
are inaccurate, as you do not
know the true reality of their
life and situation.

Say, "I Love You"

Say "I love you" often
to those you love.

Call Your Mom or Dad

Call just to chat
and see how they are doing.
Call them to say you love them.
Keep in touch
with those you care about.

Dare to Love and Love Again

If you have had your heart broken,
practice forgiveness, heal,
and have the courage to start over
with someone else.

SPIRIT

*"Religions are different roads
converging upon the same point.
What does it matter that we take
different roads as long as
we reach the same goal?"
~Gandhi*

Pray

Pray in thanks and gratitude.
Pray for the well-being of others.
Pray for the healing
of yourself and others.
Pray in faith that all is working,
as it will ultimately
benefit those involved.
Pray that the perfect answer
is revealing itself to you.

Have Faith in God or A Higher Power...and Yourself

Believe in a loving
God or Universe
who is always with you.
Have faith that all will
work out in the end.
Believe in yourself—
that you matter
and that you can
make a difference
in the world.
Have faith you will
achieve your desires.
Trust that you are enough,
you are loveable,
and you are loved.

Practice Forgiveness

Forgive quickly,
deeply, and completely.
Forgive yourself.
Forgive your enemies,
and remember that forgiveness
is for yourself,
not the other person.
Apologize
and ask forgiveness verbally,
if possible, or in prayer.
Live and model
a life of forgiveness.

Accept and Love People

Avoid being critical.
Love people
in spite of their limitations.
Realize that people
are doing the best they can
at the moment with what
they have and understand.

Don't Take Things Personally

Realize that when someone criticizes you, it is only a reflection of that person's inner problems and experiences.

Practice Letting Go

Let go of guilt, grudges, fear, anger, and any other damaging emotions that keep you from experiencing peace, joy, and love.

Be Kind and Tolerant

Use kind words
and think kind thoughts.
Show kindness to strangers.
Show kindness to
those you love.
Be kind to animals.
Be kind to nature.
Be kind to yourself.
Be tolerant of others
who have different beliefs
or physical characteristics.

Be a Thankful Person

Write thank you notes.
Send thank you cards
for gifts promptly.
Say thank you to people
you interact with during the day.
Look for opportunities
to express appreciation
and gratitude.

Practice Being
Instead of Constantly Doing

Take time out of your day to rest.
Take time to experience
silence and quiet time.
Feel what it is like to "be."
If your life feels frantic
and stressful, slow down.
Avoid the urgency addiction
of always rushing
and feeling pressure
to get things done
that may be trivial.
Don't rush through life
or wish it away.
Enjoy each phase of your life.

Take Time Each Day to Feed Your Soul

Nourish your soul with sunshine,
nature, music, pets, a hug, a kiss,
quiet time, a massage, a great meal,
talking to a friend,
or some other way
unique to you.

Watch as Many Sunrises and Sunsets as Possible

Sunrises and sunsets are the perfect time to appreciate beauty and think thoughts of gratitude. Witness as many as possible.

Recount Your Blessings and Gratitude Before Going to Sleep

As you lay your head
on the pillow, reflect on all
that happened that day
for which you are grateful.
Count your blessings
as you fall asleep.

Love an Animal

Give love and attention to a pet.
Let a furry creature be a companion.
If possible, save an animal from
an animal shelter or humane society.
Have compassion for all living things.

Spend Time in Nature

Take a break from
technology and fast-paced life
and go out and enjoy nature.
Unplug from phones and computers
on a regular basis.
Bring nature inside by
cutting or buying flowers
for your home and workplace.

Plant a Garden

Whether indoors or outdoors,
plant flowers or vegetables or both.
Create beauty or food.
Create plant life.
Plant a tree for a special occasion,
such as the birth of a child.
Nurture and care for what you plant.
Watch what you plant grow.

Be the Change You Want to See in the World

If you want peace, live peacefully
and support peaceful causes.
The only person you
can change is you.
Don't waste your time
and effort trying to change others.
Change your own attitudes and
viewpoints because when you
change your inner world,
the outer world changes.
Set an example of
truly living positive virtues and
modeling behaviors for which
you can be proud.

Savor the Present Moment

Let go of the past.
Plan for the future
but focus on the now.
All you truly have is this moment.

Always Give and Be Your Best

Be your best self always.
Give fully to your job.
Give fully to your relationships.
Give your best to each task
and every day.

COMMUNITY AND SERVICE

"If you want to live a long life, focus on making a contribution."
~Hans Selye

Support the Arts

Go to a concert, art show,
museum, theater, movie,
opera, or ballet.
Donate to the arts
and culture of your community.
Take an art class.

Leave Things Better Than You Found Them

Tidy up, clean, fix, and beautify.
Even if no one is watching or
nobody acknowledges it,
enjoy making things look better.

Volunteer

Give your time to a cause
or organization in your community
with which you feel an
alignment and connection.
Let others know
about volunteer opportunities.
Spread the word about good causes.

Vote

Exercise your right to vote.
Make a decision and cast your
vote on Election Day.
Ask people you trust, respect,
or admire about their
political opinions and positions.

AND A FEW MORE...

*"As long as you live,
keep learning how to live."*
~Seneca

Have a Definite Chief Aim

Develop a singleness of purpose
by aligning what you think, do,
and say with that purpose.
Have a burning desire for
achievement of your definite chief aim.
Focus your thoughts
and your energy on this aim.
Engage in work you enjoy
that is consistent with
your definite chief aim.

Master the Basics

Build a solid, deep, and strong
foundation for all you do.
Master the basics of your job,
communication, and skills,
practicing them over and over
until they are second nature to you.
Review this book until the suggested
principles have become a part
of your everyday life.

Avoid Multitasking

Have one focus at a time.
Your productivity is higher
with a one-task focus.
Your stress level is lower
when you have clarity of purpose.
Give your full concentration
to only one thing at a time.
Avoid wearing many hats that
diffuse your focus, time, and energy.

Make Progress

Do one definite thing each day
that ought to be done without
anyone telling you to do it.
Do at least one small action
each day that will move you
ever closer to your ultimate goal.
Do challenging tasks at
the beginning of your day.
Do one thing each day that you have
not been in the habit of doing.
Do it without the expectation of pay,
but with the desire
to be of value to others.
Do what is right without being told.
Be someone who takes action
and avoids procrastination.
Tackle the most important tasks first.

Don't Complain

Instead of complaining,
take action.
Often you are complaining
to the wrong person.
Either approach the source
of the complaint directly
or take some sort of action
to change the situation.
You may also decide
to change your attitude.
Focus on what you want
instead of what you don't want.

Gather New Ideas and Contemplate Life

Be a reader and
lifelong student of life.
Spend time in contemplation
of life and its meaning.
Engage in meaningful discussion
of life with friends.
If you live in the city,
visit the countryside.
If you live in the country,
visit the city.
Visit other countries to expand
your view of the diversity of
cultures and the human condition.

Ask for Feedback

Once you get feedback,
you can make improvements
and adjustments.
Ask others how you are doing,
how you can improve,
how you are limiting yourself,
or what you need to stop doing.
Be open to what you hear.
Make adjustments and try
new behaviors and see
if you get a better result.
Results don't lie.
If you don't like the results
you are getting,
do something different or
ask for feedback and make a change.

Develop Self-Confidence

Believe in yourself
and your abilities.
Consistently practice
skills that you need to acquire
to achieve mastery
and greater self-confidence.
Find a mentor, coach, or teacher
to guide you.

Cultivate a Pleasing Personality

Develop an interest
in other people.
Praise the good
qualities of others.
Shake hands firmly
while expressing
warmth and enthusiasm.
Smile and give others
your full attention
during conversations.

Be Decisive

Attempt to make decisions quickly.
After a prompt decision,
change your mind slowly.
Avoid indecision, as it drains
your energy and does not
move you forward in life.
Your first instincts are usually right.
Most decisions can be changed
if needed, so go ahead
and make decisions now.

Embrace Change

Change is inevitable,
and if you are constantly
growing and evolving,
change will occur in many ways.
Be open to change,
as it will open the doors to
new friends, relationships,
and opportunities in your life.
Holding onto the way you have
always done things or viewed
the world is stagnant living.
Living a dynamic life is exciting.

Ask for What You Want and Need

If you don't ask for what you
want in life, the answer is always no.
Dare to ask and you will
find that it is often given.
Be specific and clear with your requests.
Ask with expectations
of a positive outcome.
Be persistent.
If necessary, ask someone else.

Listen To and Follow Your Intuition

Trust what your gut
or heart is telling you to do.
That feeling inside prompting
you to do or not do
something is often a big clue
about the direction or course of action
that would be best for you.
Allow yourself to feel
your inner promptings.
Follow these inner feelings
when making decisions.
Be true to your heart.

Find a Teacher, Mentor or Coach

Learn from someone
who has proven to be successful
in something you want to
be successful at doing.
Ask to be a student or apprentice.
Interview those you respect and
ask them questions about how
they achieved their success.
Ask advice from those who
have come before you.

Study and Celebrate Success

Observe success.
Congratulate others for their successes.
Ask successful people questions
about how they achieved success.
Hang around successful people.
Admire and model successful people.
Read books on success.
Frequent places where
successful people hang out.
Define your idea of success
and reevaluate regularly.
Celebrate your own successes.
Understand that success attracts
success, so acknowledge your
successes, even small ones,
as they all add up.
Expect to succeed.

Live Simply

Keep your life from
becoming too complicated.
Minimize the quantity of stuff you own
and the size of your living space.
Large houses, garages,
and closets fill up fast.
Keeping your stuff simple
is freeing, and it is much easier
to move when needed.

Avoid Accumulating Clutter

Get rid of stuff that isn't useful, beautiful, or doesn't bring you joy. Sort through closets, desks, garages, basements, or any place stuff accumulates, and sell or donate anything that has lost meaning or that someone else might want or need.

Arrive Early

Cultivate the habit of
arriving early to everything.
Early arrivals reduce stress.
Arriving early respects
the time of other people.
Carry a book with you so that
you can enjoy reading
when you arrive early.

Practice Self-Control

Delay immediate gratification.
Save for big purchases.
Avoid excess.
Have a plan for how much
you will indulge at parties
and when you will leave.
Learn to say no
when your gut tells you
that a choice is not in
your best interest.

Be Courageous

Experience a full life.
Try new things,
reach out to others,
stretch your comfort zone,
speak up about important matters,
and take a stand when it counts.
It is okay to feel fear
and be aware of it,
but move beyond it to take risks
and live your full potential.
Avoid regrets by
embracing opportunities in life.

Use a Journal

Capture ideas, write notes from
inspiring speakers, set goals,
record accomplishments,
write insights, and collect wisdom.
Review periodically.

Be Cautious About Who You Listen To

Listen to people who have
what you want and have
been where you are now.
When you are learning from
others, observe if they practice
what they preach.
Are the people you are watching
modeling the principles or
values they promote?
Find and follow examples
or a mentor who lives in
integrity with their teachings.

Keep Learning and Growing

Be teachable.
Be a lifelong student.
Always seek to learn more and
be an expert at what you do.
Continue to take courses in self-
improvement and self-development.
Stretch yourself regularly by
learning something new or acquiring
a new skill or technique.
Use your car's audio system
or another listening device to
learn while you commute.
Continue your education
after graduation.

Learn Another Language

Visit the country of the language
you are learning and practice
with the people.
Encourage children to learn
another language at an early age.

Be Impeccable with Your Words and Actions

If you say you will do something, do it.
Do not make promises you cannot fulfill.
Become reliable to all who know you.
Be as good as your word.
Officially de-commit from
anything that you cannot complete.
It is better to say no than to agree
to something that you are not
certain you can fulfill.
Your character is made by you and
completely in your control
and is the sum of your thoughts,
words, and deeds.
Sound character
will lead to a
good reputation.

Practice Giving and Receiving

It is a wonderful attribute to
give to others, but it is necessary
to be a good receiver as well.
Practice being a receiver by graciously
and gratefully accepting compliments
and other gifts.
Accept such gestures
with a thank you and by not
minimizing yourself while doing so.

Maintain Your Car

Get regular oil changes,
rotate your tires,
and perform regular maintenance.
Keep your car running well,
and it will save you money
down the road and prevent you from
being stranded on the roadside.
Learn how to change a tire
or join a roadside assistance plan.
Develop a relationship
with a mechanic.

Be a Safe Driver

Do not text and drive.
Drive sober.
Avoid high speeds.
Be a courteous driver.
Wave thanks to drivers
who let you in.

Slow Down and Avoid Urgency

Accidents happen more often
when you rush.
Slow down,
take some deep breaths,
and realize that very few things
are true emergencies.
Schedule fewer things
in your day and say no
or cancel if needed.
Focus on quality not quantity.

Manage Priorities Instead of Time

Do what is most important first.
Fill your mornings with
your top priorities.
Later in the day do trivial items,
if you have time.
Avoid interruptions
of phone or email
during your productive segments.
Clean up messes in your life and
complete unfinished projects
before starting new ones.
Before you begin a new project,
ask yourself if it is really a priority and
whether it will be a benefit to your life
and to your life's purpose.

Respond Instead of React

If possible, take time before you quickly react to something or someone. Be thoughtful, and after some time has passed, respond if necessary. Change your response to achieve different outcomes if you are not happy with what you are experiencing.

Practice New Skills Instead of Trying

Mastery takes practice.
Dedicate time to practice.
To become unconsciously competent
at anything may take years of
dedicated time to hone your skill.
Practice baby steps towards your goals.
Use the word "practice"
instead of the word "try."
Do it or don't do it,
but don't "try."

Be Persistent

Never give up!
Persistence pays.
Practice one more time.
Give it another shot.

Celebrate Birthdays

Celebrate yours and others.
Send birthday cards and call
people on their birthdays.
Take someone to lunch or dinner
on his or her birthday.
Sing happy birthday to people.

Take Pictures to Capture Moments

Give pictures to others that
show them enjoying something—
like a meal, gathering,
holiday, or vacation.
Print the picture and
give it to the person
in the photo
or to someone
who loves that person.

Reduce or Eliminate TV Watching

TV is a time waster.
Consider reading instead.
Go outside,
exercise, be in nature,
or talk with people
instead of watching TV.

Add One New Good Habit and Drop One Bad Habit Each Year

Habits add up whether
they are good or bad.
Selecting one good habit to add
each year can bring you improvements
in your life over time.
Gradually eliminate
bad habits each year as well.

Practice the Golden Rule

Do unto others as you would
wish them to do unto you if you
were in the other person's position.
Think of others as you wish
them to think of you.

Leave a Legacy

Make the world a better place.
Live your passion.
Care for the well-being of others.
Find a way to help humanity,
even if it's one person at a time.

Notes

Notes

Notes

101 THINGS I WANT TO DO— MY DREAM LIST

*"If we did all the things
we are capable of doing,
we would literally
astound ourselves."*
~ *Thomas A. Edison*

☼

Have some fun
envisioning your future,
including places you would
like to visit or experiences
you would like to have.
For example, you might want to see
the Great Wall of China or the
Pyramids of Egypt.
Perhaps you would like to shake hands
with the President of the United States
or be interviewed on a TV show.

Spend some time listing a few items
now, and as you think of more,
add them to this list.
When you accomplish one, check it off
and celebrate that accomplishment.

My Dream List

1. _____ ❑
2. _____ ❑
3. _____ ❑
4. _____ ❑
5. _____ ❑
6. _____ ❑
7. _____ ❑
8. _____ ❑
9. _____ ❑
10. _____ ❑
11. _____ ❑
12. _____ ❑
13. _____ ❑
14. _____ ❑
15. _____ ❑

My Dream List

16. _____ ❏
17. _____ ❏
18. _____ ❏
19. _____ ❏
20. _____ ❏
21. _____ ❏
22. _____ ❏
23. _____ ❏
24. _____ ❏
25. _____ ❏
26. _____ ❏
27. _____ ❏
28. _____ ❏
29. _____ ❏
30. _____ ❏

My Dream List

31. _____ ❏
32. _____ ❏
33. _____ ❏
34. _____ ❏
35. _____ ❏
36. _____ ❏
37. _____ ❏
38. _____ ❏
39. _____ ❏
40. _____ ❏
41. _____ ❏
42. _____ ❏
43. _____ ❏
44. _____ ❏
45. _____ ❏

My Dream List

46. _____ ❏
47. _____ ❏
48. _____ ❏
49. _____ ❏
50. _____ ❏
51. _____ ❏
52. _____ ❏
53. _____ ❏
54. _____ ❏
55. _____ ❏
56. _____ ❏
57. _____ ❏
58. _____ ❏
59. _____ ❏
60. _____ ❏

My Dream List

61. _____ ❑
62. _____ ❑
63. _____ ❑
64. _____ ❑
65. _____ ❑
66. _____ ❑
67. _____ ❑
68. _____ ❑
69. _____ ❑
70. _____ ❑
71. _____ ❑
72. _____ ❑
73. _____ ❑
74. _____ ❑
75. _____ ❑

My Dream List

76. _____ ❏
77. _____ ❏
78. _____ ❏
79. _____ ❏
80. _____ ❏
81. _____ ❏
82. _____ ❏
83. _____ ❏
84. _____ ❏
85. _____ ❏
86. _____ ❏
87. _____ ❏
88. _____ ❏
89. _____ ❏
90. _____ ❏

My Dream List

91. _____ ❏

92. _____ ❏

93. _____ ❏

94. _____ ❏

95. _____ ❏

96. _____ ❏

97. _____ ❏

98. _____ ❏

99. _____ ❏

100. _____ ❏

101. _____ ❏

Recommended Reading

The Success Principles, Jack Canfield

The Law of Success, Napoleon Hill

Think and Grow Rich, Napoleon Hill

The Seven Habits of Highly Effective People, Stephen R. Covey

See You at the Top, Zig Ziglar

Secrets of a Millionaire Mind, T. Harv Eker

The Little Money Bible, Stuart Wilde

The Top 10 Distinctions Between Millionaires and the Middle Class, Keith Cameron Smith

Total Money Makeover, Dave Ramsey

Rich Dad, Poor Dad, Robert T. Kiyosaki

The Game of Work, Charles A. Coonradt

How I Raised Myself from Failure to Success in Selling, Frank Bettger

The Four Agreements, Don Miguel Ruiz

How to Win Friends and Influence People, Dale Carnegie

How to Have Confidence and Power in Dealing With People, Les Giblin

The Magic of Thinking Big, David Schwartz

The Magic of Believing, Claude M. Bristol

The Power of Positive Thinking, Norman Vincent Peale

You Can If You Think You Can, Norman Vincent Peale

Ask and It Is Given, Esther and Jerry Hicks

The Passion Test: The Effortless Path to Discovering Your Life Purpose, Janet Bray Attwood and Chris Attwood

The Slight Edge, Jeff Olson

The Power of Your Subconscious Mind, Joseph Murphy

Mind Power, John Kehoe

The New Psycho-Cybernetics, Maxell Maltz

Become an Athlete of the Mind, Lisa Shultz

As a Man Thinketh, James Allen

Acres of Diamonds, Russell H. Conwell

The Go Getter, Peter B. Kyne

Secrets of Longevity: Hundreds of Ways to Live to Be 100, Dr. Maoshing Ni

Connected, Andrea Costantine

Letting Go, David R. Hawkins

Power of Now, Eckhart Tolle

A New Earth, Eckhart Tolle

Man's Search for Meaning, Viktor E. Frankl

Forgiveness, Gerald G. Jampolsky, M.D.

Simplify Your Life, Elaine St. James

Don't Sweat the Small Stuff—and it's all small stuff, Richard Carlson

The Five Love Languages, Gary Chapman

His Needs Her Needs, Willard F. Harley, Jr.

1,000 Places to See Before You Die, Patricia Schultz

Oh, The Places You'll Go, Dr. Seuss

ACKNOWLEDGMENTS

Many thanks to Donna Mazzitelli, Karen Foster, Andrea Costantine, Laura Jacob, Ginny Brannon, Staci Shultz, and Ashley Shultz Griffin for your feedback and suggestions. Even small word changes make a big difference!

ABOUT LISA

In addition to being a mother of two daughters, Lisa Shultz is the co-creator of the anthology series, *Speaking Your Truth*. Three volumes of *Speaking Your Truth* were published, each with over forty women courageously sharing their stories of inspiration.

She is also the co-author of the book, *How to Bring Your Book to Life This Year,* and the solo author of *Sally's Journey. How to Bring Your Book to Life This Year* guides and supports the aspiring writer to bring their book into publication with ease and success. *Sally's Journey* is a short novel based on the true story of her beloved dog Sally, written from the eyes of Sally.

Lisa has a passion for studying and practicing the power of the mind and thoughts. She speaks to groups and has workshops entitled, *Become an Athlete of the Mind,* which is based on her book by the same title.

She lives in Breckenridge, Colorado.

Visit her website: www.LisaJShultz.com